cares a whole awful lot,

get better. It's not.

TM & copyright © by Dr. Seuss Enterprises, L.P. 2021

All rights reserved.
Published in the United States by Random House Children's Books,
a division of Penguin Random House LLC, New York.
The artwork that appears herein was first published in various books by Dr. Seuss.

Random House and the colophon are registered trademarks of Penguin Random House LLC.

Visit us on the Web!
Seussville.com
rhcbooks.com

Educators and librarians, for a variety of teaching tools, visit us at
RHTeachersLibrarians.com

ISBN 978-0-593-12329-4

MANUFACTURED IN CHINA 10 9 8 7 6 5 4 3 2 1 First Edition

Random House Children's Books supports the First Amendment
and celebrates the right to read.

Dr. Seuss's
THANK YOU FOR BEING

GREEN
AND SPEAKING FOR THE TREES

Random House  New York

I am the Lorax.
I speak for the trees.
THANK YOU
for being green.

THANK YOU
for thinking
about helping
the earth.

You care
about the
TREES ...

the **AIR** . . .

and the **WATER**.

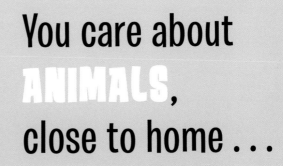

You care about **ANIMALS**, close to home . . .

and far away.

You **RECYCLE**.

You **CLEAN UP** when others litter.

You **GROW** things.

Because you are green,
our future looks brighter.
THANK YOU!